We

Met

In

Beijing

We Met In Beijing

Poems by Anthony Tao

For friends and family

Contents

II.

III.

IV.

My gratitude to the editors of the following publications,
where these poems first appeared:

The Shanghai Literary Review, "Expats in Beijing"
Eunoia Review, "Chinese Love Song"
The China Project, "Dirty Bar Street"
Rattle, "Coronavirus in China"

Here we part, friend, once forever.
You go ten thousand miles, drifting away
Like an unrooted water-grass.

—Li Bai

I landed in Beijing

February 2023

to find everything had not changed
like they said. From the jetway I sensed
a familiar austerity in the haze rising
out of double-barreled chimneys, sky smoke
flattening landscape, blurring time.
This was the city where everything, mortar
and air, grew older before their time, time
lost as easily as jade turned into stone—
and stone to jade, when time permits.
I hadn't been sure I'd miss this place,
but then I arrived at the baggage claim floor
where a door ajar revealed a converted office
with security guards resting on bunk beds.
This was the Beijing I knew, where very little
squares with what you've read.
Outside, the thin cold slipped under my coat,
through my fingers. *Drive in double time,*
I told the cab driver, *let's cut through this dust,*
and off we went through the coarse aesthetics,
leaving behind jaundiced fields, anorexic trees.
Cold doubled, smoke doubled, fortune doubled.
Industry banded together to blot out the sun.
Light in Beijing is just a glare anyway, a sheet
of diffused pale spread over carved-out streams
and flapping in wind, flicked onto windows, cracking
above coal or in the ancient firepits of memory—
the unspoken hopes, the glittering struggles.

I.

Being Someone Else

Cindy donned a dinosaur onesie
Jerry came as Mad Max

Dani wore face paint like she was in *Cats*
James squeezed into a pink dress

And since this was 2021, plenty
of *Squid Game* tracksuits and masks

Someday we'll leave it all behind, Manuel observed,
his mustache curled upward like Rich Uncle Pennybags

Someday isn't today, Arianna replied,
tugging at blue socks inside slippers dipped in red dye

The DJ spun while bodies bumped
Strange remixes from Austria thumped

How many more days and nights they'll go on like this
is anyone's guess. We cede the floor to those

who believe it never gets better than this
They're the fresh-faced, thin-boned

who look good in smart jeans or hot tights
and flirt effortlessly as saying hi

"Empire State of Mind" came on, the song by Jay-Z,
and a coterie of young Chinese

in and out of costume began mouthing
Let's hear it for New York

Let these lights inspire you
Take another shot and go go go. Go

be someone else: Dracula, Cruella, clown—
a young adult with a direction and care

Maybe it does never get better than this
No self-exams out here, just a song and a prayer

Sandstorm

Is that sun or ulcer, cancer or moon?
Silver, the smell of arsenic, shape of methane
On papier-mâché, eye of abscess
Punched into plywood.
Sky has tint, dust texture. Orchids
In these florets of spring leave hope shaded.
The city has been upset, sneezing chalk, achromic
With canker sore. How unsettling to step outside
In the bottom of our bowl, snowed under the weight
Of economy, dirt and saliva swimming, to find
Jester on the throne, tartar on the tongue, phlegm
Dried up the nose. Methane is a tetrahedral,
I know, color returns with wind, sand
Just an itinerant riding through
On a caravan of heat. Still.
Is that a sun or moon?

In the City

He was fond of saying
We'll see,
unable to commit
to noncommittal entreaties.
We can brag we're twenty-first century
modern men, *millennials,*
but the truth is we're as stupid
as the boomers,
bitter at facts, fidgeting
with ciphers and devices.
What I'm trying to say is,
it wasn't anyone's fault
that he said *We'll see*
when she asked about dinner.
The next evening, dining
over candle and cocktails,
they played their parts politely,
enthusiastically bantering and trying
hard to find the other funny,
interesting, etc. After all, they hankered
to use the other as anchor, sought
reprieve on a decision, wanting
not to know where this was heading,
not know the nowhere their lives had folded into
in a city that just might be, if they thought about it,
unhealthy for their souls. This place
has us cynical, unfeeling, or feeling
like we deserve more than we've got.
What were you doing last night? she asked, I think
implying he should have gone to her then.
I was busy, he replied. *Writing—*

as if recording one's vanity cleanses us of it.
Anything to ensure
he was not the one hurt
by her unasked question
with its implication, with an answer
he could not give:
What are you doing now?

Self-Censorship

Bosses visited. Not their first time
in China, but it'd been long enough
for them to love it. Or at least say so
on the high-speed train from Beijing
through the windmill-dappled inland
past state-of-the-art bridges and EVs
to amusement-park Shanghai. *It isn't
as I remember it*, they said. Of course
I put up with their gushing, resisted
rolling my eyes when they complained
they couldn't send a tweet. Insights
came to me—though others likely
noticed too—the insanity of $8 coffee,
of watering the asphalt, of requiring
a Chinese ID to book most hotels.
We passed a man on the street
bent over spare parts, repairing fans
for a buck-fifty. We passed empty
rows of apartments. *The economy
is at an inflection point*, they were told,
local economists and academics all
more pessimistic about the future
than they. All that glitters, I suppose.
They delighted in the craft beer,
the newly shaded alleys, cat cafés.
We drank and ate too much, cheese
dumplings and numbing hotpot,
sucking air through our teeth, ranting
on American politics and Michelin bullshit.
They added Chinese coins to their handbag
of exotic languages, alongside *ahlan,*

annyeonghaseyo, cześć.   *Tangping*
was their favorite, meaning "lie flat,"
a form of quiet quitting among
Chinese youth. *I'm glad to see*
you haven't tangping, they said
as I whisked them from subway to
construction site to Xinjiang diner,
where we talked climate. *John Kerry*
could've accomplished more, they said,
adding, *No one probably cares.*
On their final night, they paid for dinner
through an app, beaming, *I can't believe*
all the things you can do on your phone,
and, *It's about time WeChat linked*
to American credit cards. I admit
to a bit of satisfaction recognizing
the conveniences I took for granted.
And the tradeoff, what our relatives
gave up, told as they were, *Stay out*
of politics and you can get rich.
I pondered the changes I'll be first
to witness, living in this ongoing
experiment we signed up for
through a swipe and a tap. I think
I won't tell them; let them discover
the future themselves, when it arrives.
When they left, I did feel tired, in need
of a nice liedown. On my phone
I ordered takeout and watched videos
until I forgot things I wanted to say.

St. Patrick's Day in Beijing

What's the craic? The revelers were out.
The embassy's Guinness ran out
so we battered on to Paddy's,
their Chinese staff, you know, full of
sass and charming, happy and knowing
how to give the business, Katherine
buzzing to see us. Jameson and gingers
evaporated between our teeth, we took
a shillelagh to our livers, said *Keep working*
ya bastard, brogue heavy with desperately
seeking truth and beauty or whatever problems
cursing the English will tide over. Meanwhile
a donnybrook broke out between the tongue
and soul, a crowd gathered to watch Smitty's
spit get knocked out. *People in Ireland don't have to*
do that shit, Da Rou said, referring to an American
wearing green on this holiday *no one knows anything about.*
I was on the lash, my head's in bits, but who cares
—*Ganbei*, cheers and bottoms up, curse duty,
the oncoming morning, the incomprehensible
languages of spirits in flight. Shamrocks up,
curse the brain, stow away heartache, curse
the saint this day is named after, who was
British. *Oh I love too much and by such by such*
in this Irish bar owned by a Frenchman. *Sláinte*
good friends, all glasses refilled, nothing needs
remembering this day with the revelers out, joy
and desperation truth beauty whatever. We'll grow old
never or maybe when the Guinness runs out.
Through the streets broad and narrow we sang
seeing the ways Dublin and Beijing are the same.

Shannon sat on the curb and Aoife swayed
and Paul was crying for some reason. When tomorrow
tells us it's half-past way too bloody bright do we
snooze or go guns blazing, effing and blinding,
chasing snakes again till the sun Irish goodbyes?

Leaving

For Matthew Byrne

I'm going back, Matt said,
and there he was / back
in the life where he was meant
in Manchester, ex-musician married
with baby on the way, in the way life
is meant—not here / in the
deep hours of a Beijing night
across a sour IPA, baiting reply
with a vigorous stare, eager to cut down
our desperation for meaning, for
documentation / for days when we've
grown old on the seats of prefab pubs
mutilating our stories for the pleasure
of strangers but knowing
what truths / we cherish
enough to preserve. *It's the end
of Fairyland. Now we must return
to duty.* For a brief moment
I'm there with him / on the Congleton soil,
which is the pavement of a call center,
England's roots needling out of his pores,
Ireland twined around bones of the dead,
cigarette cindering between fingers,
alcohol thickening in the blood,
eyes fixed upward,
the forgotten rising like water,
clamor until / there are drums,
there is poetry, there is a stage
for us to shout everything we pray will last,

reverie and rain during some charmed spring
escapade, pique and clang and smoke and then
the painful brightness of a 7 a.m. obtrusion
through which we stumble / our ears ringing
to a dreamless sleep.

Burning

A fifth straight day above 100.
We're walking through soup
carrying the weight of extra CO_2.
Bike gears screech, paint shrivels,
old men hike up their shirts, ants
find reasons to not work. Tempers
and common sense crack too
in the cauldron. Even after the sun
has clocked out, embers smolder, wants
blister. I watched a cop jam a knee
into the neck of a facedown drunk
tossed out of a club for fighting.
Minutes and minutes and minutes
passed until onlookers no longer
looked. Cooler heads did not prevail.
When the ambulance arrived
the cop hoisted him up from his
cuffed hands as if he were a parcel.
They strapped him on a gurney
and loaded him in, all of it
feeling unnecessary, like an extra
ten degrees when we're already
boiling; when regret has registered
but the mouth just needs a second
to say I'm sorry. This was purgatory,
too late for discretion, too early
for breakfast. Soon the sun,
not properly rested, would begin
its slow ascent, lugging light
and all that, overeager. That bastard.
Really being a dick about it.

I Want It That Way

For Dan Murtaugh

Who knows how many he's had at dinner.
A couple wines in our cozy bar
and glowing chat later, his face ruddy,
he's inviting the women up to their feet
—now that Backstreet Boys is playing
and the drinks are effervescing,
yeast alive and headmashed, footloose.
The three of them circle and spin, twirl
one another at the right rhythm, then
faster, celebrating the genuine, unfaltering.
A Chinese drinker, older, takes out his camera
and chuckles. He has been nursing his wine—
pink now, white poured into remnants of a red—
for fifteen minutes, while up there, man on fire
leads on. I avert my gaze a fraction, nervous
they'll trip up, become self-conscious,
that the women will pirouette
into the ground, but what I hear instead
is a steady, sure stamping of feet, followed
by all of them now bellowing together
Ain't nothin' but a heartache...

It was one of those nights

you feel like apologizing for.
The big band was playing,
old faces and new flames
mixing like poison and venin,
gin and toxic, hunger in the blood,
delusion in the brain
while the saxophone popped
and the trombone brayed.
When the brass blasted
arpeggiated EGBs
we put our shoulders into it,
saw spirit and soulpaint,
who was desperate and who
body-blocked for friends.
The drummer waged assault,
the singer in ecstasy slayed,
the bassist nodded the beat;
they spoke to us
through waves
and when the guitarist riffed
we smiled. Midnight
rolled and the shots
said, Is it time now?
The god of want
demanded tribute
but we said Wait—
one more song.
There's no one we didn't
want to see on this
Saturday in Beijing
with the big band playing
and bodies packed in,

wearing like dandruff
the flakes of prior lives.
How do we tell others
what it was like? What future
listener will believe
the bangers we delivered,
how fun this city can be?
Worries took a backseat.
Faces, flames grew impatient
but it's not bodies we sought,
it was stories, to explain
we got lost in a thicket,
calves slashed by thorns,
ankles grabbed by vines,
but even tumbling as we were
heels upward we crashed
into the place we were headed,
a reflective pond in the jungle
of our urban playground
where all our bad choices and
our best choices waited, where
nudes and wisps smirked and
music made the water shudder.
Diplomats, journalists, scholars,
teachers, rabble-rousers, artists,
shakers, chasers and the chaste,
those with dignity and those
still searching—how do I tell you
everyone we saw, real
and imagined? How immaculate
they were. Do I tell you
how we danced?

Veld, Spoor

For Liane Halton

Night falls on the Beijing veld,
cover thrown atop concrete and glass.
           Watch the humans creep,
puff out their chests like oryx and gemsbok,
slink to their watering holes, turn paroxysmal
and spoor what they desire, eyes flashing
cheetah green, lioness yellow.
          Here in the Beijing habitat,
the treeless plateau, we are purblind
with drought-resistant livers, romping
on sweet- and sour-veld, dreaming
of succulents and jackalberry, waterbuck in stot.
In our fuddle we confuse nectar for water
and drums for thunder, throw up our arms
to receive what we believe is the holy specter.
          "Let me show you
what it's like in my home country,"
the musician from South Africa says,
and strums two chords—
               veld, spoor
                    —and suddenly
      the nightsky opens
and down pours light in a hail of heat and rain,
summer storm of phosphene and octane

—and there, the leopard in montane scrub,
the caracal in thornbush with tufted ears waiting
for who-knows-what, vulture or good luck.
          Look at the spying monkeys in the leaves,

the wildebeest rearranging dirt beneath its feet,
those mongoose darting in for a steal.
                              On the dance floor
we see through each other to the thorny aloes of our nerves,
ashamed by what we wanted.
                              We are perspecting
through God's Window the impala and baobabs,
horns and hands held by weeping lovegrass.
Our deflagrating lust turns meager, then dust.

Postcard

It is a perfect October day, white clouds
and blue sky. We don't ask for much
in Beijing, where we've been conditioned
to fear expectation, intimacy. Some cats
are littered around the house, ignoring
the construction beyond, or the beeps
of vehicles moving in reverse. Coffee
moves us forward while QQ streams Bone
Thugs-N-Harmony. *This is nice,* I say
to someone not here. They all died
when they left, proverbially, having flown
to the corners of their Ohios, Blighty, and Bays,
where they take salsa classes on Tuesdays
or down pints at the Queen's Head at five, chuffed
at last to conform.   But sometimes
a postcard appears, out of the blue,
I guess you can say, reminding me
of an old apartment where we cooked
and clambered onto the roof via window
with wine bottle in each hand, watching
fireworks blast out the old year,
thinking how it would never get better
than this, thinking we needn't put on
more than pajamas in the ancient alleys
strutting our entitlement for tourists,
thinking we could always be anything
other than what we were.
We were out of our minds, knowing
the guise of things a less careful person
might call joy. It's a nice memory,

that's all, for a thirtysomething
in a city not his, nice enough to wish
you were here.

Expats in Beijing

It was with a laugh that Jacob asked
if any of us had tried heroin.
At once you could see our breaths lightened
like balloons liberated from children.
Laurie's freckles showed, Margo tugged
on the hem of her dress, Jane
wore the expression of someone pained
to know she could not shrug "It's fine,"
and as they turned to me I cleared my throat
against this expectant hush.

It's an exhilarating sadness, a great
unburdening and climax,
and simultaneously
the journey toward it,
like drinking at the new Topwin bar.

That was a lie. Of course they believed it.
Who cared about truth or highs
since we were all playacting romantics
in the shroud of a Beijing night.
It would have been impolite to admit
the teething burdens that gnawed inside
or reveal what lonely unease kept us
pinned here to secret ambition,
what dignities cheapened, failed consummations
nourished our growth meaningfully

and which led simply to the next
rooftop party. We knew alfresco,
hot yoga, KTV, *ayi*'s, vermouth

dens and jazz lounges, which duties to abide
and which to postdate;
we envied past selves, learned helplessness,
left tomorrow to the unthought-of fates,
achieved a different form of weightlessness,
a different class of drug, I suppose,
but all the same: anything to make us forget time.

Laurie, Jane, Margo, Jacob, plus
some others, sufficiently impressed
to move to the next subject, mused
on bar closings and VPNs, who was leaving and who best
made bagels, carried Roquefort, Bleu de Gex,
tacos and beers, when to Temple and when to QS:
talk of visas, dresses, conquests, concepts—
writers who don't speak, runners who don't rush—
a simple self-destruction
by not doing.

We tried trap, we tried hashtags,
we donned costumes at Marvel premieres
and cried when reality imposed such realness
in the form of lost elections;
we glimpsed, from the distance of our terraces, how close
we were to understanding, *if only…*
—*We are the last real Americans,* someone said,
composing another newsletter to friends,
subject line *Ozymandias,* girdled by bacon
grease thick as insouciance, a feeling, faintly, of
        accomplishment.

Not that it wasn't good. It could be beautiful
in that dusty heat
like being in a movement.
"Let's go to that Topwin bar," someone suggested.
It was late and awful, the kind of hour
where nothing better, per usual, is to be done.
"Exhilarating sadness," said Jacob.
"Unburdening," said Laurie.
"New," said Margo.
"Drink," said Jane.

Laurie, Jane, Margo, Jacob, plus
other placeholders in a poem
that will never be published,
boon companions in amusement slums
where responsibilities are relinquished
and no one is good enough:
dreams wait, cars honk, blood stiffens.
We are the they living lives of us.
Someday I'll tell you
how it really was.

II.

Dancing Like a Laowai

I was ready to leave
when the clock struck midnight.
Shots way too easy
rolled in so we made a game of it:
Take one for your granny,
bless her buried heart.
Take one for your teachers,
bless them for teaching tests.
Take one for your friend,
dearly departed because Beijing
wasn't the life she wanted.
Take one for yourself,
and another if you have no car,
no apartment, no lover.
We rattled on the dancefloor
like addicts, clacking our joints
while the booze flowed.
The pretty ones twirled,
knowing how far
they were willing to be led.
Time left, we stayed.
Next thing we knew
our heads were on the ground,
music poured into the earhole,
eyes pressed shut.
Till we could hear color, smell
the shape of lust.
Rihanna. Queen. Journey.
Nothing particularly Chinese
about living our highest lives,
which we'll brag about in the morning.

What a time to be alive,
dancing like a laowai until the early light.
Didn't we have tests to study for?
In a previous life; in a wastebasket alongside
old ambitions, all their useful lies.

* *Laowai: foreigner*

Catching Snowfall

It snowed in the city so
we were good to each other
for two hours or so.

Bashfully we paused under
the miracle of erasure, the sky
lilac, the renewed trees

handsome breathing things,
stout like a secret well kept.
And our homes: argent, amber, ash.

We were pure, with
pleasure in faith,
embrace of doubt.

Soon enough we will return
to ourselves, with rancor
and the need to be right.

We'll pee in the niveous white.
We'll poison our livers,
forget to stick out our tongues.

New Year Offering

She feeds cardboard into a flame
alone in the alley corner, easy as
pressing palms together in prayer.
I don't care much about ancestors,
blasphemous as that is to admit, but
I would like to know who's on her mind,
how many names she believes
deserves remembering. Perhaps the dead
are easier to please, unlike today's children
who demand what they don't need,
or our contemporaries, gossiping to get ahead.
This government says we should have more kids
for society's sake but they don't see the society
each person carries, they don't step outside
on a night like this, the cold dense as the blackness above,
crouching to kindle a fire. The demon that dances
dances in her pupils, palms extended.
Be gracious on this festive evening, you ghosts.
Be prosperous, mother, father. I send evidence
of my happiness and wealth.

Beijing Air

Some days you wear the heat,
take the sun's thrombosis
on your skin. Other days
you taste the change, catkins
collecting on the tongue like snow.
In winter, warmed by coal,
we turn our buried-under-masks
noses and whinge about dirt,
while in autumn we complain
of chills and transience—
          How unlike ancestors
who saw the world as one
continual spring: they had *vision*,
the glint off a beauty-struck iris
or twitch of a tiger's whisker,
Zhuge Liang scenting wind.
          In later, peaceful days,
the sage would braid his digits
beneath the sleeves of his robe
and measure time by his aches.
Nature flowed through him.
He saw the colors of night embedded
in the motions of day, gray as sunrays
yellowing the haze upon painted peaks.
Just over them, he knew, swayed a blossom
of peaches.

Chinese Love Song

She is quick to giggle, riddled
with unanswered questions:

Is it *he*, him, his character?
His whiteness,

white for privilege
and power? Or that inside

he quivers?
She giggles, forgetting

her mother had said
giggling was unseemly

for such an ugly girl—
her mother was honest that way,

and nearly fainted seeing him on her arm.
Around the corner, always corners

of what she shows him,
he wonders

what she sees. Shy and unaccustomed
to attention, or being teased,

hidden chords of his body
thrum. *Yellow fever,*

buddies winked, laughing at him.
He blushes. It's true:

The heart burns to kill, as if fevered,
when it is uncertain.

My friends call me Small Eyes,
but you can call me Dana,

she said in their first meeting.
He snorted. Together,

with her giggle,
they form this song's hook, like

love love love, but
who knows. *What do you hear?*

he asked on their first night in bed.
She was too scared to say.

Maybe another day.
She'll recall picking lentils

and he'll teach her *Magic:*
The Gathering, Black Lotus manna

for Disintegrate, she a creature
immune to sorcery.

Future nights
with movies, streamed TV,

photographs on trips taken,
disagreements negotiated,

boring things, unsettling things,
other things that must be completed,

they'll find a common language.
Who knows if they'll make it.

Hopefully they remember to laugh
so their beautiful children inherit it.

Beijing Early Summer Scene

It takes twenty-six minutes from the airport
into the summer evening. Then ten paces
to feel this is where you've needed to be.
Hey there's a BBQ place with multiple taps.
There's a Shanxi diner with donkey burgers,
a Halal noodle shop with the best
smashed cucumbers, *paihuanggua*.
I think how lucky I am, able to enjoy
a pint of beer anywhere, Wuhan or here.
Tattoo parlor, grocery store, calligraphy workshop:
Learn to paint words, enter for more information,
a loudspeaker blares on repeat till we no longer hear.
There're lots of good restaurants, someone remarks
passing by. Lady you can say that again.
Coughs behind masks, loogies onto the curb.
Two young adults walk with pinkies hooked
while a mother asks her child to look ahead.
An old man on a stool with legs crossed fidgets
with a lighter in hand and shouts about Old Jin
who recently returned to the countryside.
A shit-eating grin on his face. Screw Old Jin!
We never liked him much anyway.
Probably he'd forgotten his roots.
They know to listen for insects awakening
with the dawn. They know weather, how summer
smells of prunes and winter of red dates.
They know which things have gotten better.
Coffee places are still open at seven, in case
you were wondering. But why would you
think such a thing, you not here, needed maybe

in a different countryside with your own
early summer scene. Someday we'll together
drink away strangeness, accept contradictions,
explore the limits of what we know. Friend,
I do not expect to see you, but just in case—
it takes twenty-six minutes from the airport to here.

Midsummer Rain in the Ancient Capital

Unrelenting. This city can't take it,
midsummer rain in the ancient capital
grinding mountains into mounds,
flooding the way. Pipes aren't up to it,
drains too small. And the people,
psyches fit for dryness, shrink and
fume, cancel everything. History
is written by water—avulsion, breach,
dragon fury, erasure—but it speaks
a language forgotten.   Mongols
founded this city, imagine them
sheltering at the mouth of subway
stations, standing on the top steps
of restaurants under awnings, frozen
by the cascade, the fat bombs, twisting
arrows from blanket of sterling,
torrent of slop, soak, their leather
drenched, the curved blades of their
sabers sagging, hand calluses abruptly
visible with the mud washed off,
and shoulders slumped, bearing
new weight, wet hair, slipping
headgear, disappointment. Industry
grinds to a halt, plans pause, thoughts
of stillness fester—and daydreams
of drip, gallop of water, onslaught
of rain, unrelenting,
merciless.

Modernista

After a show

The musicians step off stage
triumphant and flush,
chased by the ghost of the percussions they played,
needing no congratulations.

The notable and notorious of Beijing
have packed this bar everyone has gone to
because where else would they be?
Go on leading with the body

as if in heat, on heels
or in disappointment
into the breach, shouting to wiggle free
and succeeding, briefly,

before the next tray of shots:
Ganbei, salud, sláinte,
down the gullet and into the gut.
How you chant *One more song*

and evacuate into the electric night
with grievance, frantic for certainty.
Back inside, breaths and movements
bump, collective mass coalesces.

A Frenchman orders an absinthe
and praises Rohmer's theatrics,
a journalist speaking German
discusses lockdowns and the Olympics,

a fiction writer pops a happy pill
and speaks to the blond:
their mouths move while nothing is said.
The beehive-haired guitarist,

the drummer with four buttons
unbuttoned, the couples
eying each other, asking
if it's time. I am sensible,

says a man leaving early;
he was out too late
the night before, because
where else would he be?

Let us ravage what youth
we don't need in this city
where no one grows up.
Let us chant *One more song*

till our souls tilt, till our throats ache.
Are you happy? someone asks,
as if we didn't own our choices
made in China. As if we didn't bask

in happy days, happy hours,
birthdays, Taco Tuesdays, buy-one-get-
one-free days, in whiskey sours
and vodka on the rocks.

Where else would we rather
run out our clocks,
with bar openings and club-
goings at dawn, always

a reason to get fucked
and strut in the imperial dust,
in the metallic smoke
amongst ravishing loves,

you beauties and beasts
laughing and sulking
in Beijing's shared vanishing.
Hold me with your sway,

with one more song. The DJ is on.
Will you remember the show they played? Hold
a little longer, hold your dissenting, your disintegrating—
let us dance, reminisce, and rejoice

before our glorious forgetting.

Return

The fruit seller slicing pineapples on the curb has returned;
I thought she had left forever when those apartments burned.
The housekeeper who tried sales is back again;
I never could do anything else, she said.
The swallows are nesting;
They had not all been killed off in fifty-nine.
The blind erhu player I knew fourteen years ago
Who sat in the middle of the south side of Dongzhimen
I swear I saw in Sanlitun the other day. Apparently
Now he has a wife.
Why can't anyone leave this place
Where everyone says we're not wanted? Funny, the thing
        about that:
We all have our reasons, listening as we do to voices
        deep inside
Where our real IDs are kept.

New Club

We watched for hours, smoking till our fingertips met our
      lips,
tapping our feet outside the front door, half-listening to
      whomever speaking.

Finally, quarter past midnight, they arrived, the cool people
      of Beijing,
the fashionable in white shoes and burgundy leather,
      piercings in plush lips,

pomaded hair and trimmed beards, sharp jawlines, dimples,
      curly, burly hair,
or the unadorned, slim and unoppressed, simply cackling
      hard, the models

and TV stars, the half-Brit and mustachioed South American
      and *American*
Americans, perhaps lugging vexations like the rest of us but
      hiding it well

behind marble-blue or emerald-green eyes, or wrapped all
      tight
inside leopard-print yoga pants which sheened in light,
      flexed like skin.

A trio of Italians batted their deluxe lashes, loosened their
      rollicking tongues,
which to us sounded dangerous, with violent intent, but
      deep, too, like a bruise.

Mate, where are you from? No, I'm *Irish, you sound posh as the*
  Queen.
What do you do? Where have you been? People here are the most
  gorgeous, don't you think?

We could make ourselves understood if we really tried—
    we could smile
as wide, drink ourselves into that euphoria where bliss and
    ignorance mix

—but what we really wanted was the knowhow to sway so
    easily, joke so candidly,
flirt as if consequences were for our parents: to see a glance
    while dancing and just know.

Young women talked about the idiocy of their bosses, of
    white men.
Tall tattooed musicians hunched while waiting for
    something interesting to come up.

The perfume of the Russian we see everywhere, who rarely
    speaks and never smiles,
wafted past us. Shall we go in? an Asian-faced girl asked in
    a strange accent.

No better place than here to waste all we've got. Or meet
    someone we didn't need
but wanted. The sky's turning matte, the body's electric
    heater whirrs. Others

on the concrete linger. Maybe someone they wanted to see
    didn't show up.
Maybe their bodies were bored. Maybe they felt stuck, no
    place to belong,

or paralyzed by spirit, by the cool people of Beijing striding
    up now to this club
which just opened, the place to be, trying to pass the hours
    between midnight and dawn.

Lyrics and lust they babble with their lizard lingo—if only
    they asked: What we wanted
and what we could give. Where we'd met before and might
    again. We trudged inside

to see, along the walls, the beautiful people of Beijing giving
    each other handjobs,
rearing back their heads to laugh so brazenly we felt like we
    weren't there.

Dirty Bar Street

Sanlitun, Beijing nightlife district, mid-1990s–2017

For those who are confused, "dirty" describes the spirit:
Depravity downed with cheap liquor, virtue unused.
Alley stained with slobber, cheats, sin, chunder—that's vomit
      For those who are confused.

Good times made worse, that's what we signed up for. But
      we knew
Living gets shorter, youth never younger, and to quit
Meant missing history, our chance to say *au revoir, adieu.*

Anyway, we found friends, bit of eye candy, some wit.
Past the reaping hours, when sun-smeared haze blighted
      our view,
We marveled we were here, *this* Beijing. We took a pic
      For those who are confused.

Can I ask you something?

For someone like me,
with no education and
no skills, how would you
suggest I make money?

I don't know
what my passions are.
Maybe gaming, just
on my phone,
but I'm not good enough
to livestream.

Under ideal circumstances, a coach,
but who could let me
in the door?
Where even is the door?

How much do you make?

9,000 a month
driving from 8 a.m. to 10 p.m.
I give 6,000 to the car company
and the rest to my wife
in Hebei with our kid.
He's one. I'm twenty-nine.

Do I look younger?
Once you have a family
you're tied down. I thought
I was being responsible, but
now I know. I envy
your freedom.

There are many people
like me in China, without
prospect, no clue .
how to be part of someone
else's society. Dreams
are what people talk about
if they have ability and luck.
Tenacity pays the bills but
it is tiring.

Thank you, boss. I'll take
your advice to heart.
But I'll tell you the truth:
I think the country's just this way.
The more you want it to change, the less
you understand what it's changing for.

III.

CORONAVIRUS IN CHINA

Written February 2020

1.

In the Neighborhood

We smiled through facemasks,
said hello with our brows,
held open doors

to remind each other
we were still here. Miss Chen the grocer
was gone, back to her hometown.

Old Li the barber was gone,
along with his radio. Zhou the locksmith
only left a phone number. Min absconded

with her cherished regrets. And
the Zhang family, who made flatbread,
never returned: *Gone*

for the new year, the sign
on their door read.
Those of us still here

nodded knowingly, sidestepped
couriers zipping down our alleys
on our way to Tang's noodle shop.

The sky is nice, we grunted. The air clean.
We were surrounded by kindness that barely
seemed real. Our throats itched for coal

and tar. Whatever else we craved,
of insurrection or speaking truth
to bureaucracy, whatever small

bonuses we desired for ourselves
or ailments we nursed, of anger
or temperatures, we did it indoors.

We pulled our curtains and waited
until the kettle screeched, then said
exactly what we had always wanted.

2.

In the Streets

The viruses had first and last names
until there were too many to count.
We grafted masks onto their faces

and by that point, what did names
matter? We locked them in
boxes, sealed those boxes within

larger boxes built in ten days. But
still they leaked out into the streets,
confused, bumping randomly

into people who could not see.
Watch for them, we whispered,
but to us they all looked

the same. We practiced saying
plague, a fun word, and some of us
wished for it, because why not. Alas,

it was hard to overcome hardwiring,
animal instinct to survive even
if we knew we were doomed.

We stalked the side alleys with déjà vu
feeling we'd done this before, back
in another lifetime—spying

on neighbors, reporting family,
mantis arms and *wheels of history*,
misery enforced as baseline.

In a way, we are all the same disease.
To survive humans, you have to give up
humanity—so says the tyrant within.

Our lungs cracked like sheet ice, breath
whistled through our veins like steam. We searched
for sickness, but there was only sharpness, like guilt.

3.

In the Bedroom

The virus watched, nose pressed
against the window, but the lovers
didn't notice, they rolled like bonobos, shaking

the bed. We heard through our walls,
which means they could hear us, too,
shaking in ways animals can,

forgetting—forgiving—our limbs, our
organs, all the ways our rococo parts
can thrash, can work toward climax, can spoil,

omphalos of all the worlds where we
exist, our vigor omnidirectional.
On the other side, our other neighbor

pounded on the wall. *Damn
him*, we thought, could he not
take it up with the virus, out there?

Of course, we knew we were being
unfair. The virus was here to stay.
We could sense it even now, lonely

virus shivering in the cold,
eyes alit upon the ecstasy unfolding,
time and everything stopped, its breath

fogging up our window, trying to leave
a reminder, its mouth curled in an O,
shouting *Ooh-la-la*. And, *Bravo!*

4.

In the Imperial Garden

The virus is an enemy that fights without rules
but it lacks resolve. It lacks country.
We speak this way inside the Imperial Garden

in the Office of Epidemic Prevention
and Control to remind the people
who is in control—of who has not

abandoned them, who can lift fog,
move mountains and rivers.
What would you sacrifice for your home,

which is your country? We will discipline failures
on a pillar of shame. We will stay upbeat.
We spared a thought for the city besieged

in the province of one thousand lakes;
we heard a man leapt off Simen Gate bridge,
but truth is what we say. The poet says

truth is what's proclaimed before judgment,
but what does it matter? The good doctor
died despite believing. We do not believe—

we know how the system works, how numbers
are reported, what newscasters mean when they
stipulate faith in the Ultimate Arbiter.

"Do you understand?" is a rhetorical question.
Would you choose People *over people,*
country over self, Party over family?

We tore down mahjong parlors, demanded
whereabouts, asked others to set an example,
maintain distance, sleep in separate beds.

Be patriotic. At home, our real homes, we huddled
closer than before. We feared if—when—we came
out of this, they would see clearer than ever.

5.

In the Air

Masks. Wearing them,
we were more aware
of the other.

Our eyes locked more often,
for longer, searching for provocation,
gauging interest

down to conjunctiva.
We experimented with sounds,
soughing and snuffling,

and remembered the lessons
our cats and dogs had taught:
ears back, head tilted. We were polite

to those we did not care for,
widening our expressions,
softening our brows

to say we understand the feeling.
But occasionally, next to a body
we leaned toward,

we grimaced with yearning,
with agony and despair that we could not
rip off these masks and laugh

at our poor nerves aflutter. Our gazes
settled on cloudshadow and withy,
old tiles on rooftops and dragon wings

rippling the pale blue. We saw the ways
we merge with the world, with the air,
taking into our lungs

the trees, the purslane in pavement, the rewards
for being who we are.   *Magic,* we said
to ourselves, forgetting what we were afraid of.

6.

In the Heart

We stopped saying hello.
We infected with caprice,
infected ones we love with doubt,

those we dislike with conviction;
with memories of the gone,
which is an exacting affliction,

afflicted as we are with the same disease;
with misunderstanding,
with truth blasted out like a sneeze,

with borders we could now see,
with suspicion
and blame we no longer kept to ourselves.

The virus was gone. In those early days
we replaced it with energy and humor,
then with our sense of what is righteous,

trying to infect others.
A triumph for our country, the news trumpeted,
while we questioned if we deserved it.

We leaned away from bodies, stopped
holding doors.
We dragged our feet on office carpets,

burdened by familiar debts.
We looked mockingly on those still masked,
forgetting the ways we are infectious.

We walked the streets like sorrowful ghosts
and with two fingers rubbed our chests.
What is it that was missing?

Winter 2022

January

The stars were out. We couldn't help
but notice, all twenty or so of them,
Orion's Belt and one of the dippers.
The sky was pale, the cosmos's printer
low on toner, but the moon shone
anyway. A hunter and bull were up there
somewhere, like all the interesting people
out there, somewhere, scattered
by, I don't know, divinity or COVID.
And fate? What surprises remain stored,
locked down? It was too cold to tempt it
so we went home, where there was no one
and nothing to upset.

Watching *The Matrix* in Beijing

February

Five of us were in the bar to start,
four stayed. The others couldn't have
gone far: The Olympics are three weeks
away. People were angry as usual
in ways we didn't know. Social media
was insisting so-and-so
comment on this-and-that,
while from afar it was easy to think
here or there was falling apart;
tomorrow the news people will find
another topic. Scan the health codes
or fake it if you want, *Just go through
the motions to give us face*, the guards
bundled up to their chins seem to say
with incurious eyes. Demanding nothing
is key to thriving in 2022 Beijing,
a simulacrum we accept. *Bullet time*,
like Xi'an locked down. Your city
may be next. A woman lost her baby
because her covid test expired;
a man's heart attack went untreated
since his district was "medium-risk,"
said an app. Who programmed humans?
Long ago we ran out of outlets to vent.
Don't get me wrong, but it's easier
to take the pills. We've settled
into our modules, shunted disease
to the alleys. Fear shuffles its feet
like neighborhood fogeys who've seen

enough. Everything's fine and if and when they're not, the *new* new normal will have to do. *Is this real?* Neo asks. It's not, two of us replied.

Spring in the Hutongs

March

I'd forgotten it could be like this,
green dangling off the trees.
You can't unsee it, once
you look, the streets
canopied, the lush
leaning forward.
The young hold milk teas
and hands, dress like
the future their grandparents
feared, ripped jeans and
crop tops; the merchants
of coffee and handicrafts
show off their stock.
How spring took its time,
how it knew yet to arrive.
The 7 p.m. news touts
old leaders visiting unis
talking of Red genes, Red
blood—a Red future
for our blah blah
blah. Sit in the paling red,
the peach-blue evening light.
Let it sink in: there is light.
There it is on your skin, on
the black locust, the juniper.

Lockdown

Shanghai

As soon as it was over
we emptied into the streets,
tree-lined and otherwise,
to Lawson's and that Italian
eatery with Spritz. We
sought mistakes to make
to shock ourselves into living,
asked strangers the size
of their cage, what they thought
of that song, which foods
they craved; we flirted this way
because it was good to see
the shape lips make, forget
the anger on our tongues. We spotted
a storefront advertising 48-hour delivery
and smirked, *It'll take seven days.*
We toasted to ourselves and our
lives, knowing how conditional
living had become. All our noise,
our flaunting, our laughter
must have felt like a taunt.
Within days, weeks, we were back
in our cages, which felt smaller.
We punched rants into devices
like sending bottles to sea. Who was it
we danced with on that sticky
summer night? When briefly
we felt phosphorescent. Now
we are in a jar, flapping

where no one can hear.
Louder, then. Pans, metals,
anything to tell the world
we're fucking here.

Anything You Want to Say

May

We're not allowed inside restaurants and museums
but this alleybar serves coffee and beer from its window.
A black-and-white shepherd-terrier runs up and down
the hutong, its ears flapping, inviting us to join.
An old woman shuffles out to spectate.
You offer your seat but she says embarrassedly, No no,
I just want to see what activity they're planning.
What they're planning, a thirtysomething with long hair
tells us, is to paint their three-wheel beer cart.
Before the colors roll we can scribble anything we want
to say. Anything at all, he adds, then we'll paint over it.
What is it that any of us want to say?
Well wishes to strangers, blessings for the suffering?
You see someone has drawn in thin marker *Zero fucks*.
You write nothing. Lockdown is coming like the weather,
one turn of wind at a time, one darkening of the heavens
for each glance upward. Let it come, seems to be
our only choice. Then let us see what words gush forth
like beer from the side of a three-wheel cart.

During the summer of 2022, indoor seating in
Beijing bars and clubs was forbidden for a month.
People found other ways to socialize.

Liangma Canal

June

The lights went out around ten,
someone's idea of driving us away.
We cheered the dark, clinked beers
till noise rose from the promenade.
Drink vendors zipped by in scooters
hawking Coronas, their idea of funny;
others slung hard stuff, gin and Beam.
No one had anywhere better to be,
not even the cops, content to watch.
And then droplets appeared, unseen
but cutting cleanly through the heat,
synchronizing some of our yearning.
Look up, look around, behind. Look:
On the svelte-black skin of the water
tiny mouths gasp for air.
Underneath, what rousing pleasure?

Moonrise

July

Swear it used to be lower
The Moon
On this rooftop bar called Moonee

The Drum and Bell hovers like a creep
The China World Trade Tower leers
At no one in particular. Who out there wants to hear

From us anyway on this terrace during COVID and fear
Or some approximation of it
Seeking fun, or some approximation, half-exposed limbs

Wiggling under specks of grime and satellite
The Earth is upside-down. We could fall to freedom
If we believed in it

We could be saved
Looking up at the ground dropping beneath our feet
If we wanted it

The Moon rises, fades
As we think on how we will never age never
Leave this place

Beijing Cough

August

It was hard to say—hard
but also pointless—how
it started. It spread: It
spoke, wrapped around throats
and squeezed, causing eyes
to water, spittle to fly. It said
Take me in, let me preach.
              Somehow
the wee bugger survived
in our summer of masks
and vigilance, jumping
from nose and mouth
to nose and mouth, orating
not the dry exegeses of
particulate and soot—
yesteryear's "Beijing cough"
—but the triumphant, wet
allegories of communion,
the conjoining of voices,
solos linked and rising
like chorus, cacophonous.
It's going around, we said,
because so were we,
evangelicals of an old order
with our defenses down,
reshaping our environment
as easily as breathing.
              We capered
and caroused, then shared
what we could of remedies:

ginger tea, a long nap, a good
sweat bath. How we missed
all this, life's subtle reminders
of mortality, believing normal
meant we lived without
conditions. As if the piper
had forgotten, and we could
enforce our own price.

Grandmothers Playing Cards

September

I'd already cycled past them
when I stopped to look back.
Two elderly women sat
around a small table, cards in hand.
Stunning, the only way to describe
the woman's hair, white as a rabbit,
and captivating, how the other
flipped through card after card
as if sorting letters from
the boys in Korea. I'm far yet
just close enough to hear
the first woman say *Lost again*
as she reaches out to shuffle.
The September sky is a wafer blue
puffing clouds of white. I think
on my own grandmothers, gone
two decades now, give or take;
I think on when my own parents
will sit like this, waiting for grandkids
who may or may not arrive.
It all comes back to us, doesn't it,
by which I mean the anxious, petty,
solicitous, wide-eyed, considerate and
keen, empathetic and earnest
little you inside, processing age
and time, loneliness and being alone,
love and living. What do they mean,
these two old women in Beijing,
how is it they've insinuated themselves

into the story of your life? As she finishes
her shuffle and begins to deal,
I hope, for all our sakes, that she gets
the hand of a lifetime,
and then again
and again, odds be damned.

Looking Back at the Pandemic

October

I'll remember the small oddities, how
the oldest amongst my neighbors
went unmasked, and the sounds
autumn makes, every bit of the season
calling for recognition we couldn't give
sitting inside with our screens, hoping
each day might lead somewhere other
than where we were, our brains
perpetually elsewhere: on an island,
atop a mountain, in a plane sailing
over white billows of locomotive steam
into a future delayed, leaving behind
a past we someday, per normal, will mourn
—when greeters waited at every building,
by the river and by the beer window;
when "scan the code" replaced *hello*;
when we were more attentive to movement,
sensitive to change: how fast it happens,
when it happens in China, as if nothing
had ever been out of the ordinary.

Peace, Prosperity, Longevity

The new year

My neighborhood barber says every hutong
lost three or four during those months. Elders,
preexisting conditions, those on their last straw.
Mostly. Another winter that history will forget.
I pause at my door to look for Old Zhang the cat lady.
I keep an eye out for Old Meng who wore his pants
above the stomach. And the woman with hair
bright as newfallen snow. At least Old Liu
is still here, still not saying hi. 70,000 to 80,000,
the barber estimates, gone. They don't count them
anymore, not in the supermarkets or concrete squares
where dances make onlookers curious (and envious),
not the canteens where we belch our lungs out,
chewing with mouths open, nor the offices
where we quietly quit. The red character for *fortune*
is pasted on our doors to welcome the Year of the Rabbit,
for peace, prosperity, and longevity. Life
still needs to be lived, they say, so we'll live
live *live*. And remember, for as long as we do.

IV.

We Met in Beijing

2008-2020

We met in a bar called Great Leap
It was ironic but not really

We threw dice in the dive joint Smugglers
The shots were cheap but our dignity was cheaper

A place called Heaven imported bottles of beer
Patrons picked fights while saying cheers

El Nido was where French and Americans gathered
They hated one another, but only when sober

The Den showed the World Series, rugby, football, cricket
It was the worst of haunts, but also the best

Someone died in Taco Bar after too much tequila
That's a secret we've agreed to forget

We spent New Year's Eve singing with Mongols at Jianghu
Overhead, the throat-yell of a sky splintered, of joy and
      dread

I wish you could have seen those fireworks
I wish you were there for that fire at Four Corners

At Paddy's, lads gossiped like schoolgirls, glasses were
      never empty
Whether in sonas or sorrow, we returned for the company

We took dates to Mai, Mao Mao Chong, Atmosphere
East Shore for jazz, Blue Note to impress

Ichikura stocked Japanese single malts
Q-Mex served margaritas with perfect salt

Amilal was frequented by blabbering literati
Unfortunately, its owner despised Han Chinese

We roared with laughter at Penghao Theater
On Halloween, zombie Raydens chummed with Harry
        Potters

Fubar, with its bookcase door, was the first speakeasy
One-kuai mojitos ruined it, because cool doesn't last in
        this city

For a bit, the concoctions at Apothecary were great
Anyway, Janes and Hooch snagged the accolades

Cuju served rum, then tried to be a vermouth den
When what we most savored was camaraderie in that hutong
        caravan

Mado was where a literary arts collective was founded
We went for the poetry…we went for absinthe

We watched the Super Bowl at Tim's Texas Bar-B-Q
It ran into property trouble; then again, who didn't?

People donned armor at Knights and Merchants
Drank mead and battled in a tree-lined alley

Brits in Luga's cussed with riffraff and mates
Queens sashayed down Anchor's skimpy gray runway

Everyone whispers of how it used to be, of Half and Half
And a litany of fine things that couldn't last

What does that say about those who stayed?
What were we waiting for if not change?

Capital Spirits sold cocktails made with baijiu
The Wall Street Journal liked them, but, c'mon, it was baijiu

Slow Boat, Jing A, Arrow Factory, and others
A hit list for AB InBev, which can go straight to Hell

Boxing Cat came from Shanghai
As this is a poem about Beijing, no more will be said

Maggie's was infamous for Mongolian hookers
Also, a Filipino house band that played wicked covers

At Botany and Revolution we chatted up bartenders
Mostly we just wanted a drink that didn't end

Fang Bar kept searching for a stable home
Like all of us, wandering in circles. And where exactly is
        home?

We stumbled along Dirty Bar Street, past First Floor, before
        it became a mall
Bar Blu, Pink, Red Club, White Rabbit—the colors sort of
        blended

We cavorted on Sanlitun rooftops: Kokomo, Migas, Martini
They were overrun by college kids, hedonists, beer pong
      athletes

Mix, Vics, West—jive, groove, press
Elements, Playhouse, Spark…who can remember the rest?

Lantern was an underground club for trance and techno
Corpses emerged in mornings dazed and hollow

We packed into La Social like dancing sardines
So many creeps…so many beauties

Debauchery and ogling happened in Propaganda
The body's movement was the lingua franca

Destination had a fountain and a reputation
Secret trysts and ecstasies you can't imagine

We stamped our feet on the tables of Café de la Poste
And if that was closed, there was always QS

During spring the catkins fell. We picked them off
      our chuan'r
And chugged tallboys till the world made sense. This
      was true happiness

The Local used to be Brussels, Side Street replaced
      Ron Mexico
Frost became That One Place. But who really broke
      the mold?

Outside Dada, bleak and dark, a staircase led to nowhere
We got lit there. That's probably all that I should say

Ganja and giggle smoke spelt doom for Dos Kolegas
"Performance art" got DDC closed for half a year

D-22 launched indie careers, YugongYishan and Mao
        Livehouse were the shit
Sadly, none of them made it

Chocolate had a Russian dwarf guarding the door
We visited at late hours to feel fatalistic

Sorry if I've left your favorite out
Q-Bar, Salud, Wiggy Jiggly's, The Bricks

All those hotel lounges with fancy terraces
All those Ladies' Nights that left you transfixed

The Tree, Groovy Schiller's, XL, Hidden House
Or that apartment bar, that hole in the wall you told
        no one about

During the Great Brickening we lost so many
Mas, Cellar Door, Hot Cat, and more

Closures felt like cataclysm even when they weren't
Peiping endured, as did the Great Outdoors

At least there were jam sessions at Soi Baochao, punk rock
        at School
At least there's Modernista, where we flirted like fools

Rain cascaded in sheets one summer night; we filibustered
        in Temple
Till dawn cleared the skies

During autumn, the cold infiltrated our bones. We shivered
        on scooters
And clutched loved ones till the world made sense. This
        was true happiness

The Bookworm was the nexus of intellectual life
How it survived, no one knows. And then it didn't

And when we had nothing left we could say
Outside 7-Eleven, empty Yanjings at our feet

That's when I knew I was nearing my end of days
What are we waiting for if not change?

We met in a bar called Great Leap
Eventually, even it will cease to be

"We are all renting an experience," its owner told me
He left China for good during COVID-19

Someday we'll all depart with just a memory
Either that or liver disease

Tiki Bungalow, Nanjie, White Knights, Lush
They're still around, I think. And so are we

For now. For however long, let's live forever here in Beijing
When it's time, leave behind a story

About the author

Anthony Tao was born in Beijing, grew up in Overland Park, Kansas, and graduated with a journalism degree from Northwestern University. He returned to Beijing in 2008 to cover the Olympics for *ESPN The Magazine*, and then stayed. He has worked an assortment of editing and writing jobs, captained and coached Ultimate Frisbee teams, coordinated the Bookworm International Literary Festival, owned a hutong bar, and hosted events ranging from World Cup-style beer pong to monthly poetry readings for the Spittoon Literary Arts Collective. His poetry has appeared in *Rattle, Prairie Schooner, NPR, Frontier, The Cortland Review*, etc. He is a founding member, with Liane Halton, of Poetry x Music Band.

anthonytao.com

The primary typeface used in this book is Bell MT.
Janson SSi is the secondary typeface.